IMAGES
of America

WORLD WAR II
SHIPYARDS
BY THE BAY

ON THE COVER: In all, the U.S. government spent more than $9 billion to build ships in the Bay Area during the war. And of those ships, the tankers built by Marinship in Sausalito were the most complex. The tanker *Mission San Francisco*, Marinship's 93rd and final ship, is seen here on September 18, 1945, just before it was launched into Richardson Bay. The ship's bow art reads, "Well Done," a phrase that applies to hundreds of thousands of workers who built ships and ship components in the Bay Area. (Bechtel.)

IMAGES
of America

WORLD WAR II
SHIPYARDS
BY THE BAY

Nicholas A. Veronico

ARCADIA
PUBLISHING

Published by Arcadia Publishing
Charleston SC, Chicago IL, Portsmouth NH, San Francisco CA

Printed in the United States of America

Library of Congress Catalog Card Number: 2006934440

For all general information contact Arcadia Publishing at:
Telephone 843-853-2070
Fax 843-853-0044
E-mail sales@arcadiapublishing.com
For customer service and orders:
Toll-Free 1-888-313-2665

Visit us on the Internet at www.arcadiapublishing.com

"Ships for Victory" was the slogan the U.S. Maritime Commission used to motivate war workers into delivering maximum production. As shipbuilding goals were achieved, workers received "Ships for Victory" pins. (Author's collection.)

CONTENTS

ACKNOWLEDGMENTS

Shipbuilding dominated the Bay Area shoreline and was a tremendous contribution to America's war effort. Thousands of families in the region worked for or supported the Bay Area's shipbuilding industry. As they worked, their labor was documented on film by company photographers as part of the shipbuilder's contract with the government. Those images now reside in a number of archives, both public and private. Companies and organizations granting access to their collections in support of this work included the City of Alameda Library, the Bechtel Corporation (operators of Marinship), The Iron Man Museum (Joshua Hendy Iron Works), Navsource.org, Oakland Museum of California, Oakland Public Library, Richmond Museum of History, Sausalito Historical Society, South San Francisco Public Library, SS *Jeremiah O'Brien*, and the Vallejo Naval and Historical Museum.

In addition, a number of individuals went out of their way to assist the author. A debt of gratitude is owed to Margaret and Tony Badger, Darryl Baker, Clementina and Donald Bastin, Martha Bergman, Caroline and Ray Bingham, Hannah Clayborn, Scott Davis, Desirae Fromayan, Richard Grambow, Kevin Grantham, Capt. Walter Jaffee, Kathy Kay, Jim Kern, Don McDonald, Michael H. Marlow, Merle Mauroni, Vickie Nichols, Jack Perry, Stan Piet, John Pullin, Chet Robbins, William Stubkjaer, Christopher Tassava, Karen and Armand Veronico, Kathleen and Tony Veronico, Betty S. Veronico, Paul Yarnall, Stacey Zwald, and the staff of Arcadia Publishing.

If you have or had family members that served in the Merchant Marine (1775 to present) and would like to learn more, visit the U.S. Maritime Service Veterans website at www.usmm.org.

—Nicholas A. Veronico
San Carlos, California

Workers from shipyards in Southern California came to the Bay Area to help fill shortages in certain labor skill categories. California Shipbuilding Corporation identification card 91920 was issued to the author's late grandfather Nicholas Veronico. Working as a welder, he would commute from his home in Los Angeles to work in the Permanente Metals Yards—three weeks on and one week off. When working at the Richmond Yards, he slept in a garage that had been converted to accommodate six men. (Author's collection.)

INTRODUCTION

During World War II, the U.S. Maritime Commission spent $13 billion on the construction of merchant ships, half of which—approximately $6.3 billion—was allocated to build ships at West Coast shipyards. In addition, the U.S. Navy spent $18 billion on its shipbuilding program, of which $2.4 billion also went to the region's builders.

Shipbuilding on the West Coast was distributed among Los Angeles, Portland and Vancouver, Seattle and Tacoma, and the geographic center—the San Francisco Bay Area. The Bay Area also had the largest concentration of shipbuilding, reaching from the Golden Gate nearly a hundred miles east to Stockton. Within the Bay Area, 14 shipyards turned out new vessels for the war effort: Basalt Rock Company of Napa; Bethlehem, San Francisco and Alameda; Barrett and Hilp (Belair), South San Francisco; Hunters Point Naval Shipyard; Mare Island Naval Shipyard; Marinship, Sausalito; Moore Dry Dock, Oakland; Permanente Metals-Richmond Yard No. 1; Permanente Metals-Richmond Yard No. 2; Kaiser Company's Richmond Yard No. 3; Kaiser Cargo's Richmond Yard No. 4; United Engineering, Alameda; and Western Pipe and Steel, South San Francisco. A number of minor yards—such as Fulton Shipyard of Antioch and William F. Stone Company of Oakland—and dozens of local businesses supported the shipbuilding industry. Most notably, the Joshua Hendy Iron Works of Sunnyvale, California, supplied engines for Liberty and Victory ships.

While Mare Island and Hunters Point Naval Shipyards built military ships ranging from submarines to cruisers, Bethlehem and Western Pipe and Steel built attack transports, seaplane tenders, and destroyers, and converted freighters into escort carriers for our allies. However, it is the construction of thousands of Liberty and Victory ships—some in only a matter of days—that captured the public's attention.

War in Europe began September 1, 1939, more than two years before hostilities touched American shores. With Britain and France facing a numerically superior enemy, the British Merchant Shipbuilding Commission came to the United States to have ships built to supplement its fleet. The U.S. Maritime Commission, which had been established in 1936, did not want to build what it considered Britain's slow, obsolete, coal-burning ships. The British were seeking 60 ships, known as the Ocean Class and based on the J. L. Thompson and Sons-designed and -built *Dorington Court*.

Existing shipyards at the time were at capacity working for the U.S. Maritime Commission, and with war on the horizon, no yards would soon become available to accommodate the needs of the British. The British gave two 30-ship contracts to Todd Shipyards, which would build the ships on the East Coast, and to Henry J. Kaiser's Permanente Metals Todd-California Shipbuilding Corporation. To accommodate the order, Permanente Metals would construct a new shipyard in the mudflats of San Francisco Bay at Richmond.

Bay Area shipyards brought women and African Americans into the workforce for the first time—by the tens of thousands. While the shipyards were being built and the majority of able-bodied men were off to war, recruiters were crossing the country in search of workers willing to relocate to the West to build ships. Most were still trying to recover from the hard economic times of the 1930s and were willing to work, and the shipyards provided training. Marinship in Sausalito and the Kaiser-controlled yards in Richmond ran three shifts a day. Special ferries, bus lines, and commuter trolleys were organized to bring workers from the cities to the outlying areas where the shipyards were located. For many, wartime work in the Bay Area became a life-changing opportunity.

Propaganda played a significant role in boosting morale, selling war bonds, and starting friendly rivalries between production plants. Kaiser's Oregon Shipbuilding Company of Portland, Oregon, built a 10,000-ton Liberty ship in only 10 days. Henry Kaiser challenged the Richmond Yards to do better, and although thoroughly planned and pre-staged, Richmond Yard No. 2 delivered the Liberty ship SS *Robert E. Peary* in seven and a half days. The construction of the *Peary* is a shipbuilding record that stands to this day.

The Allied Forces' victory over the German and Japanese brought wartime shipbuilding to a close. Thousands lost their jobs, although most would never return to their pre-war homes, as they chose to settle in the Bay Area. Many found work converting ex-military ships into merchant vessels, and many of the same workers converted the wartime Liberty ships and Victory tankers built in the Bay Area in their new peacetime professions.

Shaft and propeller destined for Yard No. 2's *Lewis Morris* are assembled in the prefabrication area. Named for New York's delegate to the Continental Congress and a signer of the Declaration of Independence, *Lewis Morris* was delivered on June 19, 1942, and operated by American President Lines during the war. The ship survived the war and was stored in the Suisun Bay reserve fleet. It was scrapped in 1961. (Richmond Museum of History Collection.)

One

Henry Kaiser Brings Shipbuilding to Richmond

With war on the horizon for America, the U.S. Maritime Commission needed a freighter—quickly. It decided to modify the Ocean Class design to ease construction and change the powerplants to oil fired rather than coal burning. The new ships were designated as EC2 (The first letter stood for "Emergency," the second letter represented the ship type—Cargo, Tanker, Passenger, and the third character gave hull length in 400-foot increments—the numeral "2" denotes a ship greater than 400 but less than 450 feet in length). Additional letters and numbers following dashes indicated the type of powerplant, number of screws, and modifications made to the ship. Having a new design and a definite need for new ships, the U.S. Maritime Commission contracted with Kaiser's Oregon Shipbuilding Corporation and Bethlehem-Fairfield Shipyard, Inc. to build the new emergency-cargo ships that would make up what was called the "Liberty Fleet."

As Kaiser built additional yards on the West Coast, he exchanged his East Coast interest in Todd Shipyards for complete control of the Todd-California yards. With his clean break from Todd, Kaiser's Permanente Metals began building ships for the U.S. Maritime Commission on the ways where the British Ocean Class freighters had been constructed became Richmond Yard No. 1. A new six-way yard, later expanded to nine and then twelve ways, became Richmond Yard No. 2—both of which were owned by Permanente Metals. Kaiser and his "Six Companies" partners (W. A. Bechtel Company, Bechtel-McCone-Parsons, General Construction; J. F. Shea Company; The Utah Construction Company; Morrison-Knudson Company; MacDonald and Kahn, Inc.; and Pacific Bridge Company from a number of dam and other construction projects) owned shares in Permanente Metals Corporation. Many of these same companies were involved in various wartime construction ventures. As the war progressed, a third yard (Richmond Yard No. 3, managed by the Kaiser Company) to build troop transports and a fourth yard (Richmond Yard No. 4, managed by Kaiser Cargo Company) to build frigates, tank-carrying landing ships, and baby Liberty ships were added to the Richmond complex. The partners of the Six Companies had an interest in these yards as well.

The Kaiser Richmond conglomerate recruited workers from as far away as New York, Louisiana, and the northern Midwest. The shipyard-worker influx changed the small town of Richmond overnight. For the war effort, trailer camps were set up, extra rooms were rented, and garages were converted into bunk houses. In all, four Richmond shipyards would deliver 747 ships, 519 of which were Liberty ships, the last being the SS *Benjamin Warner*.

Ocean Vanguard, first of the Ocean Class freighters built for the British, was launched on August 16, 1941, from Yard No. 1. Ocean Class ships displaced 10,100 tons and were powered by a coal-fired, 2,500-horsepower engine capable of driving the ship at a maximum speed of 11 knots. Note the British and American flags hanging from the ship's bow. *Ocean Vanguard* was torpedoed by U-515 on September 13, 1942, near Trinidad. (Richmond Museum of History Collection.)

Ocean Vigil was sponsored by Mrs. Henry J. Kaiser, and is seen in the San Francisco Bay upon delivery on November 13, 1941. Construction of the ship took a little more than four months from keel laying (April 23, 1941) to launching (August 31, 1941). *Ocean Vigil* survived the war to serve under the Panamanian flag. It was scrapped in 1963. (Richmond Museum of History Collection.)

Permanente Metals' Yard No. 2 began life as a six-way yard in 1941. Subsequently expanded to nine and then twelve ways, the yard is seen here operating at full capacity in January 1945. After launching, ships were moved to the three outfitting docks at the right side of the photograph, where six ships could be completed simultaneously. Note the prefabrication sheds above the ways, and the dredge working in the bottom of the photograph. (Richmond Museum of History Collection.)

Richmond Yard No. 3 began construction in 1942 with five dry docks being built versus ways. This yard concentrated on building C4 transports (C4-S-A1) of the General Class. The ships displaced 13,552 tons fully loaded and were 522 feet, 10 inches long and 71 feet, 8 inches in beam, with a draft of 30 feet. Powered by 9,000-horsepower steam-turbine engines, they had a top speed of 17 knots. (Richmond Museum of History Collection.)

This is an aerial view of all yards in the Kaiser Richmond complex, looking west, in November 1944. When the war was over, 747 ships had been built at the Kaiser yards, and the city of Richmond had grown from a pre-war population of 23,600 to more than 93,700 by 1943. (Richmond Museum of History Collection.)

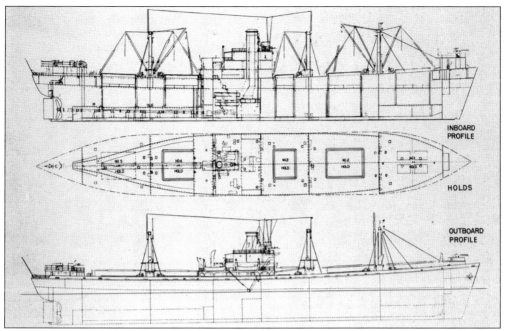

This Liberty ship three-view drawing shows the layout of the ship and its holds. Waterline in outboard profile shows the ship fully loaded. (Author's collection.)

With war clouds on the horizon and the need to expand defense-production capabilities, Pres. Franklin D. Roosevelt signed Executive Order 8802, known as the Fair Employment Act, on June 25, 1941. The order prohibited racial discrimination within the U.S. defense industry. After it was signed, a tremendous number of African American workers from the South and Midwest migrated to the defense industries along both coasts. (Richmond Museum of History Collection.)

Shipbuilding enabled women to enter the workforce en masse. Women worked as welders, electricians, and at other labor-intensive jobs. In February 1943, about 14 percent of all production workers at the Richmond yards were women. Of the African American female workers, 63 percent worked as welders or welder trainees. In spite of the economic opportunities afforded to female shipyard workers, they encountered discrimination from their male counterparts. (Richmond Museum of History Collection.)

The latest safety attire for female shipyard workers included the complete uniform, left, and the plastic bra (form-fitting chest protector), which was demonstrated to show the latest ways to prevent occupational accidents among female workers. The shortage of skilled labor during wartime put pressure on employers to improve worker safety, while employees were constantly warned about the loss of production caused by absenteeism. (National Archives, 28-0979M.)

Taken near Yard No. 2's Shipway Seven, this photograph of the labor department's day shift shows the racial and gender mix typical of all shipyards during the war. Minimum wage for shipyard workers on the Pacific Coast was set at $1.12, with higher pay for more skilled laborers. (Richmond Museum of History Collection.)

Pictured here is Richmond Shipyard No. 2 as seen from Easter Hill looking southwest. More than 20,300 housing units were built in Richmond by the federal government during the war. Aside from the government-built housing, trailer parks sprang up around the city, and many residents rented rooms or converted garages to help accommodate the influx of war workers. (National Archives, 40-163M.)

Although enough government housing was built to house 60,000 people, it just wasn't enough. In 1940, at the start of the war, 23,642 people made their homes in Richmond. Two years later, more than 90,000 people were fighting for space. (National Archives, 12689-2.)

A 14-mile extension to the Key System Railway was built between Richmond and Oakland. Known as the "Shipyard Railway," it was built using surplus components; the cars came from New York's Second Avenue El and were converted for use on the Key System, and disused track was pulled from sites all along the West Coast. In addition, a spur was run out to Oakland's Moore Dry Dock shipyards. (Author's collection.)

California Steel Products, also located in Richmond, built subassemblies for Kaiser-built ships. Here a double bottom section destined for a "pint-sized Liberty" (Ship type C1-M-AV1) is completed on December 15, 1943. Pint-sized Liberties were used for short-haul runs among islands in the Pacific. (Richmond Museum of History Collection.)

Everything was prefabricated to speed up shipbuilding on the ways. Here entire midships deckhouses are being assembled in the fabrication buildings of Yard No. 2. Aft deckhouses with 20mm-gun tubs are being built in the foreground. (Richmond Museum of History Collection.)

This is an aerial view of the preassembly area of Yard No. 2, looking east from around Way Nine. Prefabricated sections came from the shops at left and moved toward the top of the ways. Roofed structures enabled workers to assemble sections while being somewhat protected from the elements. (Richmond Museum of History Collection.)

Dinah Shore and Bing Crosby were just two of the many notables to launch ships during the war. Also, the appearance of movie stars guaranteed an increase in war-bond sales. Shore is about to launch SS *John R. Park* at Yard No. 2 on February 20, 1943. Unfortunately star power does not always guarantee safe passage, as this ship was sunk in the English Channel on March 21, 1945, by U-399. (Richmond Museum of History Collection.)

Singer and actress Lena Horne prepares to launch SS *George Washington Carver* at Yard No. 1 on May 7, 1943. The ship was subsequently acquired by the U.S. Army and after the war was modified to troopship configuration and used to carry war brides home from Europe. Stored from 1947 to 1963, the ship was scrapped at Oakland, California, in January 1964. (Richmond Museum of History Collection.)

Employees of Kaiser's four Richmond shipyards received copies of *Fore'n'Aft* on a weekly basis. The publication carried safety tips, articles about the yards and their workers, and reports from the field by sailors and merchant mariners aboard Richmond-built ships. The September 10, 1943, issue commemorated reception of the Maritime 250 Club flag for delivery of 250 Liberty ships delivered by Richmond Yards No.s 1 and 2. (Author's collection.)

One of the war's ship-engine manufacturers, Joshua Hendy Iron Works of Sunnyvale, California, was honored by the U.S. Maritime Commission with Hull No. 1696. Built in Yard No. 1, the ship was christened on July 20, 1943, and was configured for animal transport, making it capable of carrying more than 1,000 horses or mules and more than 75 support personnel. *Joshua Hendy* sat in the Wilmington, North Carolina, reserve fleet from 1948 until it was scrapped in 1964. (Joshua Hendy Iron Works, JH-1630.)

As the *Irvin MacDowell's* slide into the sea comes to a halt, the keel plate for the Liberty ship *John Morton* is swung into place on Maritime Day, May 22, 1942. At this point in time, Yard No. 2 could assemble a ship—from keel laying to launching—in about 60 days. Both the *Irvin MacDowell* and the *John Morton* were powered by engines from Joshua Hendy Iron Works, and both survived the war to be placed into reserve fleets on the East Coast. Both ships were scrapped in the early 1970s. (Author's collection.)

Pictured is a parchment certificate noting David P. Barton's purchase of war bonds during the Second War Loan. *George Berkeley* was launched at Yard No. 2 on June 2, 1943, and delivered later that month on June 14. The ship served until January 1947, when it was laid up in the Astoria, Oregon, reserve fleet. *George Berkeley* was stored until 1960, when it was towed to Kobe, Japan, and scrapped. (Author's collection.)

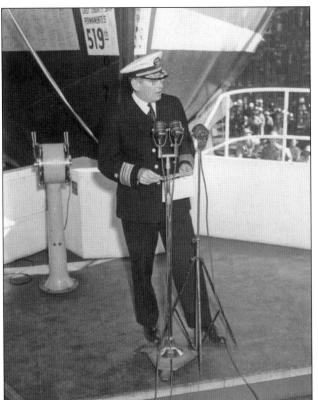

Adm. H. L. Vickey, second in command at the U.S. Maritime Commission, addresses Yard No. 2 workers prior to the launch of Richmond's 519th and last Liberty ship, the *Benjamin Warner*, on July 1, 1944. The yard had converted to Victory-ship production a few months earlier. (Richmond Museum of History Collection.)

To entertain the workers, shipyards put on a number of productions throughout the year. As school got under way in the fall of 1944, the Oakland Technical High School choir sang before some 10,000 shipyard workers. (Oakland Public Library.)

In the wartime tradition, as one ship slid down the ways, the keel plate for the next ship was lowered into place. Here, in the fall of 1944, the keel is laid for the next Richmond-built Victory ship. (Richmond Museum of History Collection.)

Bunting is hung from the bow of Richmond's 558th ship, the *Red Oak Victory*, in preparation for its November 1944 launch. The ship is named for the Iowa town that lost 27 men from Company M, Iowa National Guard during the battle for Kasserine Pass, Tunisia, in February 1943. By war's end, 50 men from Red Oak, population 5,600, lost their lives, the highest per capita loss of any U.S. city. (Richmond Museum of History Collection.)

Sponsor Edna Ray Reiley breaks a bottle of champagne across the bow of the *Red Oak Victory* on November 9, 1944, while Matron of Honor Orpha Berens protects her eyes from the flying liquid. (Richmond Museum of History Collection.)

The *Brevard* (AK-164) was launched from Richmond Yard No. 4 on November 18, 1944. Built as a "Baby Liberty" (C1-M-AV1), the ship was acquired by the U.S. Navy on February 19, 1945. It spent its military career sailing among the Philippines and the Caroline, Marshall, and Marianas Islands. At the conclusion of hostilities, the *Brevard* supported American troops in China and was involved in rescuing more than 4,200 Japanese from the sinking *Enoshima Maru*, a repatriation ship. It was sold surplus in 1947 and is believed to have been scrapped in 1970. (Richmond Museum of History Collection.)

USS *Spindle Eye* was also a Baby Liberty and was launched on May 25, 1945, from Kaiser Yard No. 4. Note the gun tubs and life-raft launchers on deck. This ship was later acquired by the Military Sea Transportation Service and renamed USNS *Sgt. Curtis F. Shoup* (T-AG-175) after the staff sergeant who won the Medal of Honor in combat near Tillet, Belgium, fighting the Nazis. (Richmond Museum of History Collection.)

Landing Ship Tank (LST) 484 was launched on January 2, 1943, at Yard No. 4, and is seen here on February 23 at the outfitting docks. *LST 484* participated in the invasions of Kwajalein and Majuro, Eniwetok, Saipan, Tinian, and Okinawa. (Richmond Museum of History Collection.)

The *Beltrami* (AK-162) was launched at Richmond Yard No. 4 on September 26, 1944, and commissioned by the U.S. Navy on January 4, 1945. It left for the Pacific theater on February 19 and shuttled cargo among the Admiralty, Caroline, Marianas, and the Philippine Islands. It, too, subsequently sailed to China to support occupation operations until January 1946, when it returned stateside. (Author's collection.)

Yard No. 4 built 15 LSTs (LST 476-490) between October 1942 and April 1943. LST 482 is seen here on March 20, 1943, under the command of Lt. R. L. Eddy (USNR), as the ship departs Richmond. The ship saw service in the Gilbert Islands, at Hollandia, during the capture of Guam, and at Leyte and Luzon in the Philippines. (Richmond Museum of History Collection.)

Patrol escort *Albuquerque* (PF-7) became an international ship. Launched at Yard No. 4 on September 14, 1943, the ship became part of the Pacific Fleet's Escort Division 27. From April 1944 to June 1945, the *Albuquerque* was manned by a U.S. Coast Guard crew patrolling the Northern Pacific and Bering Sea. After the war, the frigate was leased to the Russians from August 1945 to November 1949. In February 1953, after serving with the U.S. Navy during the Korean War, it was decommissioned and subsequently transferred to the Japanese navy—its original enemy. (Richmond Museum of History Collection.)

The war took its toll on Bay Area–built ships. The *John A. Rawlins* was launched at Richmond's Yard No. 2 on November 27, 1942. During fighting in the Pacific, on June 17, 1945, off the coast of Okinawa, the freighter was struck by an aircraft-launched torpedo and severely damaged. Three months later, still off Okinawa, the ship was blown ashore by a typhoon. The *John A. Rawlins* was a constructive total loss. (Author's collection.)

ROBERT E. PEARY
KEEL LAID 4 DAYS LAUNCHED
NOV. 8, 42 NOV. 12, 42
12:01 A.M. 3:30 P.M.
15 HOURS
26 MIN.

Although it was a publicity stunt, and one that will probably never be repeated, Richmond Yard No. 2 launched a Liberty ship, the *Robert E. Peary*, in 4 days, 15 hours, and 26 minutes. The ship was then completed and delivered to the U.S. Maritime Commission in only 2 days, 22 hours, and 57 minutes, setting another record. The total time spent—from keel laying to being fully loaded and ready for service—was 14 days, 1 hour, and 9 minutes. German propaganda called this shipbuilding feat a hoax. (Richmond Museum of History Collection.)

Two

SETTING A RECORD
ONE SHIP IN FOUR DAYS

In addition to the yards in Richmond, Henry J. Kaiser owned the Oregon Ship Building Corporation on the Columbia River at Portland. This yard built the Liberty *Joseph N. Teal* in a record 10 days—from keel laying (September 13, 1942) to launching (September 23)—with delivery three days later. A reporter asked Kaiser for his thoughts about the 10-day accomplishment, and he remarked that it could have been done in eight days, but was delayed to enable President Roosevelt to attend. With approval from Roosevelt, the decision was made to construct another ship in half the time. Plans were made to prefabricate as much of the ship as possible at Richmond's Yard No. 2 and preposition it for workers to build at the most efficient pace.

At 12:01 a.m., on November 8, 1942, a Sunday, work began with the keel laying of Yard No. 2's 47th ship. The Liberty would be named the SS *Robert E. Peary* in honor of the American explorer considered to be the first person to reach the geographic North Pole, which he did on April 6, 1909. After the keel was laid, the bottom shell unit was installed, followed by the inner-bottom unit, which holds the boiler, engine, and pump foundations. By mid-morning, the port and starboard boilers had been lowered onto the hull. Transverse bulkheads were installed, and the shaft tunnel was the last item installed, which happened at midnight.

The second day began with the installation of the lower forepeak, followed by the second deck unit and more bulkheads, and at the end of the day, the fantail was lowered to the hull.

The *Robert E. Peary* resembled a ship by the third day. The aft deckhouse, and the mid-ships deckhouse (installed in four sections) were added to the hull. The following morning, the fourth day, the forward gun platform, two masts, and the inner-stack were added by 3:01 p.m. The next 26 minutes were filled with speeches in preparation for the launch.

On November 12, at 3:27 p.m., Mrs. James F. Byrnes, sponsor, christened the ship, and it then slid into the San Francisco Bay. Launching the ship in four days, 15 hours, and 26 minutes set a world record. Delivering the *Robert E. Peary* on November 15 set an additional record for shipbuilding—taking just 7 days, 14 hours, and 32 minutes from keel laying to delivery. This was a shipbuilding feat that has never been topped, nor does anyone ever expect it to be.

The bow of the *Robert E. Peary* is prepared for installation on the Liberty ship at Yard No. 2, as seen here on November 8, 1942 at 11:30 p.m. (Permanente Metals Corporation.)

Preassembly of the stern section was completed on November 6, 1942, and moved into position for installation after the keel was laid in two days time. (Permanente Metals Corporation.)

The ship's boilers were also pre-positioned to enable the gantry cranes to lift the propulsion unit into the ship. This section was installed between 3:30 and 4:06 a.m. on Sunday, November 8, 1942. (Permanente Metals Corporation.)

Thirteen hours into the record attempt, on November 8, 1942, at 1:00 p.m., looking from the bow to the stern, workers had completed the keel and double bottom and installed the boilers, engine, and forced-draft blower. The turn of the ships hull is visible between the two sections. (Permanente Metals Corporation.)

On November 8, at 6:00 p.m., work was continuing into the night. Yard lights and crane lights illuminate the scene as the last inner-bottom unit and the final feet of the shaft tunnel are installed. (Permanente Metals Corporation.)

On November 9, 1942, at 5:15 a.m., workers installed the fantail unit. Notice the propeller-shaft alley, lower center of photograph, extending to the rear of the ship. (Permanente Metals Corporation.)

The third day, November 10, saw the *Robert E. Peary* change from hulk to the point where it began to look like a ship. Here the first mid-ship deckhouse section begins its flight from the subassembly area to the deck of the ship. Installation took nearly 30 minutes, from 4:59 to 5:27 p.m. All of the upper deck and installation of the aft deckhouse was also completed by the end of the day. (Permanente Metals Corporation.)

Nearly complete, *Robert E. Peary* awaits its sponsor and launching ceremony on Thursday, November 12, 1942. (Permanente Metals Corporation.)

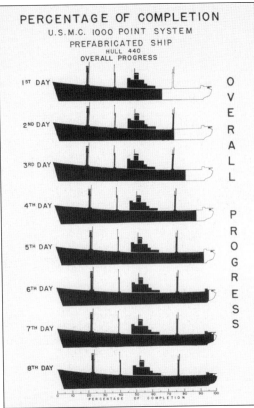

PERCENTAGE OF COMPLETION
U.S.M.C. 1000 POINT SYSTEM
PREFABRICATED SHIP
HULL 440
OVERALL PROGRESS

1ST DAY

2ND DAY

3RD DAY

4TH DAY

5TH DAY

6TH DAY

7TH DAY

8TH DAY

OVERALL PROGRESS

PERCENTAGE OF COMPLETION

Pictured here is a progress chart showing the percentage of completion of the *Robert E. Peary*. The U.S. Maritime Commission accepted the ship on Sunday, November 15, 1942, just 7 days, 14 hours, and 23 minutes after the keel was laid, which was an additional shipbuilding record for Kaiser Richmond. (Permanente Metals Corporation.)

Sponsor Mrs. James F. Byrnes, christens the *Robert E. Peary*. Mr. Byrnes was a senator from North Carolina, and was appointed to the U.S. Supreme Court in 1941. The following year, he stepped down to accept Pres. Franklin D. Roosevelt's appointment as director of the Office of Economic Stabilization, and subsequently to take charge of the Office of War Mobilization and Reconversion. The ship sponsor's matron of honor was Mrs. S. Otis Bland, the wife of a congressional representative from Virginia. (Permanente Metals Corporation.)

Amid much fanfare, the nearly complete *Robert E. Peary* slides into the San Francisco Bay on November 12, at 3:27 p.m. After its acceptance, the ship was operated by the Weyerhaeuser Steamship Company. Its first voyage departed on November 22, 1942, to the Pacific theater—first to Noumea, New Caledonia, in the South Pacific, then to the island of Guadalcanal. By April the following year, the *Robert E. Peary* had sailed to the Atlantic, where it would operate for the remainder of the war. (Permanente Metals Corporation.)

After its launching, the *Robert E. Peary* went on to see service in the Pacific and to ply the dangerous convoy routes of the North Atlantic. The ship brought back prisoners of war from the battles in North Africa and was attacked by German bombers during the D-Day landings at Omaha Beach. This ship was withdrawn to the Wilmington Reserve Fleet in December 1946 and was scrapped at Baltimore, Maryland, in 1963. (Permanente Metals Corporation.)

While crews drove more than 25,900 pilings for the shipyard, additional laborers were building the ways and piers for the yard. Shipway pile driving began on the morning of May 20, 1942, and was complete by August 19. Way Six was furthest along, although not finished, on June 27, when the keel for the *William A. Richardson* was laid. (*The Marin-er* via author's collection.)

Three

MARINSHIP'S
LIBERTIES AND TANKERS

The U.S. Maritime Commission needed cargo ships—fast. Existing yards sufficiently produced ships required for service in 1941, but demand increased in 1942. On March 2, 1942, the W. A. Bechtel Company of San Francisco was invited to propose a new shipyard that could launch ships before the year was out. A site at Sausalito in Marin County could accommodate six ways and could be built for an estimated $9.3 million. Bechtel's proposal was approved 10 days later, on March 12.

Bechtel assigned the design and engineering of the new shipyard to the Bechtel-McCone-Parsons Corporation, and MacDonald and Kahn, Inc.; Morrison-Knudson Company; J. H. Pomeroy Company; and Raymond Concrete Pile Company were added as partners. Henry J. Kaiser declined to join the venture. The operation was incorporated as W. A. Bechtel Company, Marin Shipbuilding Division, which was changed to the Marinship Corporation in November 1942.

The yard was originally contracted to build Liberty ships. As the yard was being constructed, keel blocks for the ships were added as every foot of the ways were completed. Six Liberties were on the ways, and after the sixth slid into Richardson Bay, the first T-2 tanker keel was laid. Marinship lengthened its ways to covert from building cargo vessels to building oil tankers. In all, 15 Liberties were constructed, the first christened *William A. Richardson*, the namesake of the bay facing Marinship. The company built a dozen ships its first year.

The Mission and Hills tankers were complex ships to build. Each incorporated 16 miles of pipe, requiring 17,000 welds. For each tanker, the yard's pipe shop was required to make 5,300 cuts and 5,700 bends to facilitate 5.9 million gallons of liquid cargo.

Approximately 15,000 people on payroll kept the yard in peak operation. Those workers built the T-2 tanker *Huntington Hills* in record time. The keel was laid down on May 14, 1945, and four days later, more than 2,750 tons of steel had been welded. At the 13th day, the ship was halfway done. It took 28 days from keel laying to launch and another five days at the outfitting docks, resulting in delivery of the tanker in a total of 33 days. It sailed on June 17. Marinship was truly the nation's "Tanker Champ."

As the war drew to a close, the yard built a number of barges and was planning to build floating breakwater components, known as "Dagwoods." Two additional tankers were scrapped on their ways when their contracts were cancelled on August 15, 1945. Marinship built a total of 93 ships, and its last ship, the *Mission San Francisco*, carried the bow art: "Well Done."

Richardson Bay and the mudflat that was to become Marinship rest peacefully in this March 3, 1942, photograph. More than 3 million cubic yards of Richardson Bay would have to be dredged for the launch basin, outfitting docks, and ship channel. (*The Marin-er* via author's collection.)

Work began on March 18 to convert the shore of Sausalito into a shipyard. Pine Point was dynamited, and most of its 838,763 cubic yards of dirt were used to fill in the mudflat. (*The Marin-er* via author's collection.)

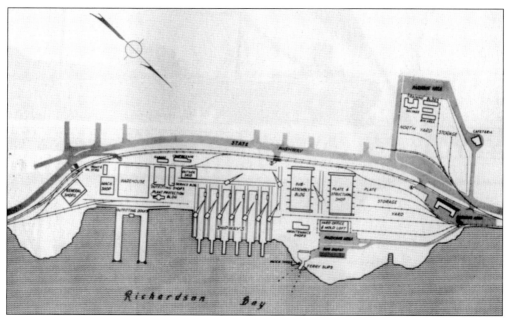

Pictured here is a map of the Marinship yard printed in early 1945 and showing the layout of the ways and the location of the outfitting docks, warehouse, shops, assembly buildings, and storage yards. Note the North Yard Storage across the highway, where the training building and reclamation buildings were located. It's interesting to note that the Plant Protection Building is shown in the wrong location, as it was located parallel to the last way and extended over the water. (*The Marin-er* via author's collection.)

Marinship executives share a prelaunching moment with Henry J. Kaiser, right. Pictured from left to right are Kenneth K. Bechtel, president; William E. Waste, general manager; Felix Kahn, of MacDonald and Kahn, Inc.; Robert Driggs, administrative manager; and Kaiser. Kaiser, Bechtel, and Kahn were part of Kaiser's Six Companies consortium. (Bechtel.)

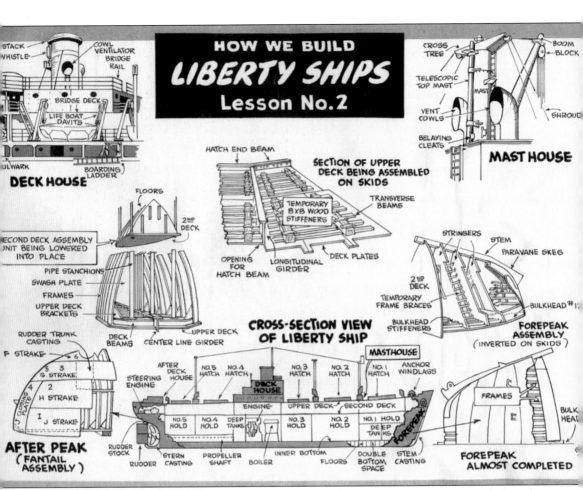

The shipyard's employee publication, *The Marin-er*, was full of useful information, including this quick-glance, how-to diagram for trainee shipbuilders. Note that most subassemblies are built upside down, or on their side for ease of construction. (*The Marin-er* via author's collection.)

To commemorate the yard's first launching, a special pamphlet was produced, giving the yard's history, details of the ship, and information on the yard's management. The first ship's name, the *William A. Richardson*, had been added to the cover photograph by a graphic artist. (*The Marin-er* via Author's collection.)

Marinship's first Liberty, the *William A. Richardson*, floats on Richardson Bay, north of the Golden Gate Bridge just after launching on September 26, 1942. The ship was named for the sailing captain and later landowner who founded the port of Sausalito and is the namesake of the bay on which it sits. The *William A. Richardson* was sailed until April 29, 1948, when it was placed into reserve at Mobile, Alabama. It was scrapped in 1969. (Author's collection.)

The Marin-er for November 16, 1942, featured a worker in silhouette watching the *William A. Richardson* head for the Golden Gate Bridge and off to war. The ship was delivered to the U.S. Maritime Commission 51 days ahead of schedule. (*The Marin-er* via author's collection.)

Goals for the yard's first year included the launching and delivery of six Liberties during the balance of 1942. Although all ships shown were launched in 1942, the *Philip Kearny* and *Thomas Hart Benton* were not delivered until January and February 1943, respectively. (*The Marin-er* via author's collection.)

Pictured here is the Marinship yard in full operation during the fall of 1944, with six ships on the ways and eight tankers at the outfitting docks (located at the bottom of the photograph). The large, flat-roofed structures in the center of the photograph are the subassembly shop and the plate shop, with raw-steel receiving just beyond. The large building to the right of the shops is the mold loft. Housing dormitories for shipyard workers are located in the top area of the photograph. (Bechtel.)

This is a view of the shipways, the subassembly shop and the plate shop, looking over housing built for the Marinship workers. (Mauroni Collection.)

Pictured here is the exterior of the 107,640-square-foot yard office (first floor) and mold loft (third floor). The large staircase on the outside of the building was used to lower patterns from the third floor for transport to the plate shop. (Marinship/Grambow, Pullin Collection.)

The 35,000-square-foot third floor mold loft was the largest clear-span space in Northern California. Here large patterns could be laid out on paper and converted into wooden templates for the shops. (Marinship/Grambow, Pullin Collection.)

The second floor contained hundreds of draftspeople needed to convert and modify ship construction plans for use within the yard. This building exists today and has been converted into office space. (Marinship/Grambow, Pullin Collection.)

Located across the highway, a training school was set up to teach new hires the fine art of shipbuilding, including welding. Today this former shipyard school serves the Sausalito community. (Marinship/Grambow, Pullin Collection.)

The yard hospital moved into the plant-protection building, next to Shipway Six, in October 1943. At the yard's peak, in the fall of 1944, the hospital treated nearly 500 cases a day, mostly eye injuries, bruises, and broken bones. During the shipyard's nearly four years of service, the hospital staff saw 478,132 patients. (Marinship/Grambow, Pullin Collection.)

Injured workers went directly to the treatment room, without waiting in line or filling out forms. The yard hospital's philosophy was to render treatment first and ask questions or fill out forms later. This reduced the loss of productive time and enabled staff to place workers in lighter duty jobs rather than sending them home. (Marinship/Grambow, Pullin Collection.)

The machinery-storage building was located near the south end of the yard and encompassed 12,300 square feet. (Marinship/Grambow, Pullin Collection.)

The yard's warehouse covered 122,500 square feet and was the main receiving point for everything a ship would need, except plate steel and machinery. Railroad tracks ran along the raised dock area. The rear side of the warehouse faced the outfitting docks to reduce travel distance for parts needed to complete each ship. (Marinship/Grambow, Pullin Collection.)

Five lunch counters were set up in the yard (at the main gate, mold loft, south end of the outfitting dock, south gate, and at Way Four). For those off shift or with business in the north yard, the cafeteria was open for a hot meal. (Marinship/Grambow, Pullin Collection.)

At Marinship, a box lunch could be purchased for 35¢, a pint of milk for 11¢, and a cup of coffee was only a nickel. (Marinship/Grambow, Pullin Collection.)

The post office for the workers' dormitories was located across the highway near the north yard. Single workers could reside here, while Marin City, across Highway 101, was built to house large numbers of workers with families. (Mauroni Collection.)

Ferry and bus service dropped workers off at the north end of the yard, near the mold loft. Ferries carried workers from the San Francisco Ferry Building and the Hyde Street ferry terminal for 10¢ each direction. More than 1,800 people rode the ferries each day, and classes were often held for workers during the trips. Bus service saw ridership peak at 3,300 coming and going to San Francisco, Marin, and Sonoma Counties. (Mauroni Collection.)

This is a publicity photograph of female chippers working on the midships deckhouse at Marinship. Chippers were highly skilled, and most female workers started out as welder trainees and progressed up the ranks in every shipyard craft. (National Archives.)

The high point for female workers, such as the welder pictured here, at Marinship was from October 1943 to July 1944. Statistics for December 1943 show 4,023 women on the payroll (23.3 percent of all workers), with the highest number (1,201 or 39.33 percent of all female workers) serving as welders. (Mauroni Collection.)

Men and women could and did work side by side in the shipbuilding business. (Mauroni Collection.)

Spectators watch a noon boxing match from preassembled bulkheads stacked at the end of a shipway. Workers were given a number of morale-building activities each week. (Mauroni Collection.)

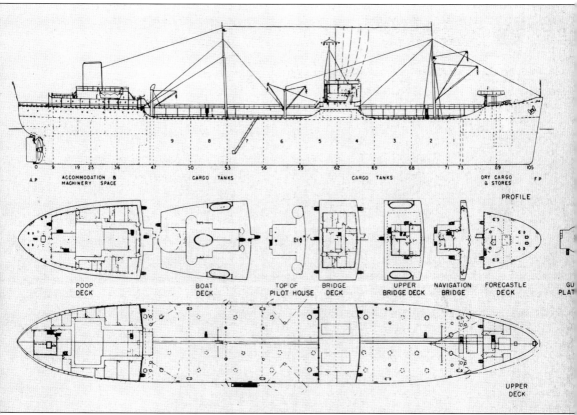

PROFILE

0 9 19 25 36	47	50 53	56	59	62	65	68	71 73 89 105
A.P. ACCOMMODATION & MACHINERY SPACE		CARGO TANKS				CARGO TANKS		DRY CARGO & STORES F.P.

POOP DECK — BOAT DECK — TOP OF PILOT HOUSE — BRIDGE DECK — UPPER BRIDGE DECK — NAVIGATION BRIDGE — FORECASTLE DECK — GU PLAT

UPPER DECK

Pictured here is a three-view of a 10,000-ton, 140,000-barrel T-2 tanker as built in the Marinship yards. Seventy-eight tankers were built on the yard's six ways. (Marinship/Bechtel.)

With the keel laid and double bottom installed, transverse bulkheads are fitted to a tanker hull. Additional shell plating is being lowered into place. (Mauroni Collection.)

A tanker's engine bed comes together in the subassembly area. This section will be lifted into the ship after the double bottom has been installed. (Mauroni Collection.)

Deck sections are preassembled before installation. Note the huge cement block being used to bend the metal structure at the right so it can be welded to the crossbeams. (Mauroni Collection.)

A 10,000-horsepower, main-propulsion motor is lifted by a gantry crane using a strong back for installation into a T-2 tanker. (Mauroni Collection.)

Marinship was building ships 24 hours a day, six days a week. The greater majority of the graveyard shift was men, with a 15¢-per-hour shift premium paid to those who worked while others slept. All shifts were 8 hours with a paid, 30-minute lunch break. Here a midships deckhouse undergoes finishing touches during the graveyard shift. (Mauroni Collection.)

Marinship riggers prepare a gantry crane hook for a heavy lift. (Mauroni Collection.)

Four gantry cranes are used to lift a 97-ton, T-2 tanker midships deckhouse. Two cranes lifted the deckhouse from the preassembly area. Then a second pair of cranes took the load and delivered it on top of the tanker's hull. (Mauroni Collection.)

Nearly 13 miles of pipe were required to outfit a T-2 tanker. That figure equals more than 1,000 miles of pipes in the 78 T-2s built by Marinship. Piping a tanker took 11 percent of the total time required to build the ship. (Mauroni Collection.)

USS *Pamanset*, AO-85, an Escambia Class fleet oiler, was laid down on March 30, 1943, and launched on June 25, 1943. It is seen at the south outfitting dock in July 1943. This ship supported operations in the Central Pacific, including the invasion of Iwo Jima, and later operations off the coast of Japan. (Mauroni Collection.)

Having sent its last Liberty ship down the ways, this July 1943 photograph shows tankers and fleet oilers under construction. Notice the size of the yard crane moving in front of the ways, as compared with the gantry cranes moving alongside the shipways. (Mauroni Collection.)

Abraham Lincoln, the great emancipator, peers down from the bow of Hull 35, SS *Mission San Luis Rey*. Its keel was laid on October 15, 1943, and it was launched on January 29, 1944. Operated by Pacific Tankers, Inc., the T-2 carried fuel to U.S. troops and bases overseas. Acquired by the navy on October 23, 1947, it served as Fleet Oiler 128 (AO-128) until it was sent to the Beaumont, Texas, reserve fleet in November 1957. The ship was scrapped in October 1972. (Mauroni Collection.)

This interesting view of the preassembly area at Marinship in February 1944 shows how the yard and gantry cranes gained access to the hulls. As Hull 34, *Mission Solano*, nears completion, parts for the next ship are prepositioned at the head of the way. Note the ship's bow and bulkheads in the foreground. Hull 33, to the right, is *Mission San Rafael*. (Mauroni Collection.)

Hours after the keel was laid for *Coyote Hills* on Way Two, the bottom plates have been installed, and they await the double bottom. (Author's collection.)

Twenty-seven days later, *Coyote Hills* awaits installation of the forepeak and bow sections. (Author's collection.)

At 57 days, the tanker, in this case USS *Pasig*, looks like a ship and is nearly ready to launch. Anchors are in place and rigged, and workers are concentrating on the oil-tank hatches. Note that the bow art has been painted just below the hull number. (Author's collection.)

The following day, July 15, 1944, *Pasig* is ready for its trip down to the sea. It only took 58 days from keel laying to launch for this 21,880-ton tanker to be built. The ship would spend another 98 days being outfitted. Mrs. John A. McCone, partner in Bechtel-McCone, was the ship's sponsor. (Author's collection.)

It was a Marinship tradition to add bow art to each tanker before launching to commemorate the sponsor or an event. The men and women of engine supplier Joshua Hendy Iron Works of Sunnyvale, California, were honored with bow art on *Buena Vista Hills*, the 64th ship launched at Marinship. (Joshua Hendy, JH39916.)

For the launching of *Mission Santa Clara* on May 18, 1944, National Maritime Day and its depiction of the sidewheeler SS *Savannah* were shown on the bow. (Bechtel.)

Hull 26, *Mission Santa Cruz*, honored the California redwoods that surround the mission. The ship was launched on September 8, 1943. (Bechtel.)

Mission San Luis Rey's bow art commemorated the contributions of American railroads to the nation's shipbuilding efforts. *Mission San Luis Rey* slid into Richardson Bay on January 29, 1944. (Bechtel.)

The likeness of Fleet Adm. Chester Nimitz adorned the bow of the *Santa Maria Hills* for its March 19, 1945 launching. (Becthel.)

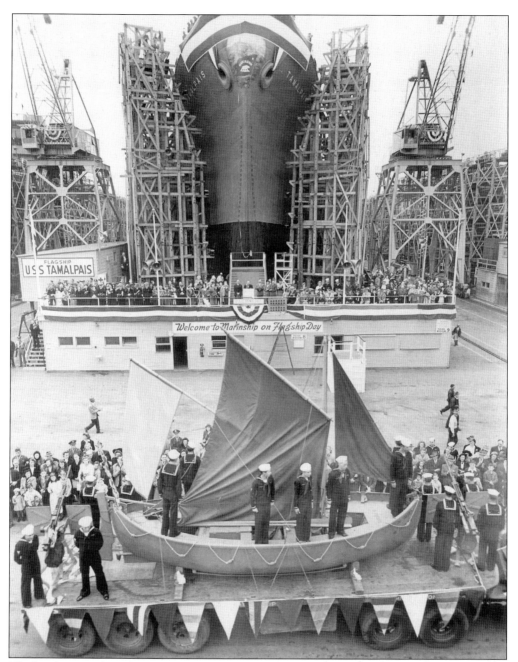

The local Sea Cadet troop entered this float for Marinship's Flagship Day, October 29, 1944, when the USS *Tamalpais* (AO-96) was launched. The bow art depicts Mount Tamalpais and shows the Marinship flag. *Tamalpais* was fitted to carry freshwater, and it delivered its first load to troops at Eniwetok Atoll in the Marshall Islands on July 8, 1945. The ship subsequently delivered supplies to the Philippines and was anchored in Tokyo Bay on August 10, 1945. (Bechtel.)

U. S. MARITIME COMMISSION LIBERTY SHIP

S. S. JACK LONDON

FIFTEENTH LIBERTY SHIP LAUNCHED BY
MARINSHIP CORPORATION
SAUSALITO, CALIFORNIA

Keel laid on June 16, 1943   Launched on July 16, 1943
Total time from keel laying to launching: 30 days

SPONSOR   MATRON OF HONOR
MRS. ANN PENDLETON DOUD   MRS. CARROL V. JOHNSON
Welder on Swing Shift   *Wife of Swing Shift Machinist*

LAUNCHING PROGRAM
8:10 P. M., FRIDAY, JULY 16, 1943

Welcome . . . . ALBERT WEBB, formerly Swing Shift
Superintendent

"Song of the Victory Fleet" . NICHOLAS CRESCI, Plate Shop Leaderman,
Swing Shift, accompanied by
JOAN WHITNEY, Marinship Secretary

Raising of Flag . . . . . Boy Scouts of Troop 33, San Francisco, under
supervision of WALTER McCONOLOGUE,
Shipfitter Leaderman

"The Star-Spangled Banner" . Led by MR. CRESCI

Invocation . . . . CHAPLAIN LESLIE C. KELLEY, Oakland

Introduction of Honored Guests R. W. ADAMS, Employee Relations Manager

*Introduction of Matron of
Honor and Sponsor* . . . . MR. WEBB

Response . . . . MRS. ANN PENDLETON DOUD, Sponsor

Launching Procedure . . . Explained by BILL WOODS, Hull Division
Inspector, Swing Shift

Launching of the S. S. JACK LONDON, 8:30 P. M.

•

THE STORY OF JACK LONDON

John Griffith London (1876-1916) is famed as the author of many exciting
adventure stories, including "Call of the Wild" and "Sea Wolf." He lived the
same daring life of which he wrote, in the arctic North and upon the sea.
Throughout the world he is best known for his vigorous espousal of socialism.
Born in San Francisco, this boy was always his home. He died at his ranch in
scenic Valley of the Moon, in Sonoma County.

The last Liberty ship launched at Marinship was the *Jack London*. Invitations were sent to shipyard workers and local dignitaries for the July 16, 1943, launch. Note that the entire launching ceremony only took 20 minutes, as the yard workers on duty needed to return to the task at hand. After the war, *Jack London* sailed for Honduran, Panamanian, and Italian ship lines. (Author's collection.)

Pictured here is a Marinship-tanker christening at the moment of impact between the ship's bow and a bottle of champagne. (Mauroni Collection.)

Launched as the Escambia Class Fleet Oiler *Lackawapen* on May 19, 1943, the ship was commissioned by the U.S. Navy as USS *Cahaba* (AO-82) on January 14, 1944. *Cahaba* supported all the major carrier air strikes in the Central Pacific during late 1944 and early 1945, and was at Okinawa during the heavy Kamikaze attacks. The Military Sea Transportation Service operated the ship until 1958. (Bechtel.)

Hull 39, SS *Mission Carmel*, enters Richardson Bay on March 28, 1944. Mrs. W. B. Lardner, wife of William Branson Lardner, a prominent citizen in California's gold country, sponsored the ship. (Mauroni Collection.)

Marinship's Outfitting Dock featured an elevated roadway that enabled trucks and carts to get closer to the ship's decks to deliver pipe and the myriad additional parts needed to prepare a ship for war. The elevated section was removed after the war. Note the proximity to the general warehouse at right. (Mauroni Collection.)

Originally laid down as the *Mission Santa Ana*, Hull 52, USS *Soubarissen*, sits along side the outfitting dock eight days after launch. Note that the deck rails are two-by-four boards and that the bridge wings have not been added to the midships deckhouse. (Author's collection.)

Ten days later, Hull 52 is making progress and a gun tub has been set on the rear of the aft deckhouse prior to installation (compare to ship at right). Although the deck looks a shambles, there is actually order there. It took 114 days to outfit this ship. (Author's collection.)

Forty-five days later, the ship begins to look like a combatant with the installation of gun tubs. Forward piping is being strung along the deck to service the cargo tanks. (Author's collection.)

By day 56, the Marinship logo has been removed from the stack and the lower deck railing is visible. (Author's collection.)

Hull 52, USS *Soubarissen* (AO-93), steams under the Richmond-San Rafael Bridge with a navy crew on board in January 1945. This ship was also fitted to carry freshwater and supported all of the naval battles in the Pacific during the spring and summer of 1945. (Vallejo Naval and Historical Museum.)

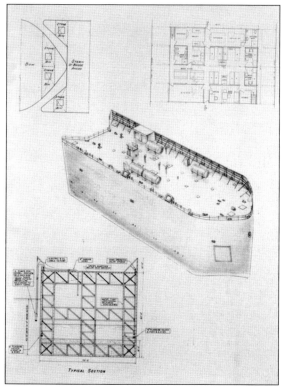

In July 1945, Marinship received a contract to build "Dagwood" barges. Each was 230 feet long, 75 feet wide, and 60 feet deep. The steel barges were designed to form a breakwater, much like the Mulberry breakwater used during the D-Day invasion. Dagwoods would be used to form artificial harbors off landing beaches during the coming invasion of Japan. The dropping of the atomic bomb cancelled this program, and none were constructed. (Marinship/Bechtel.)

The 93rd and final ship, the *Mission San Francisco*, looses way in Richardson Bay on September 18, 1945. The war was over, and Marinship's workers were to return to their normal lives. Many sought jobs in the local naval shipyards, where repair and overhaul work would sustain their careers for a few more years. The majority of the workforce was immediately let go, while a skeleton crew stayed behind to close down the operation. (Bechtel.)

By June 1946, the scaffolding was gone, and so was the hustle and bustle of 24-hour-a-day ship construction. Marinship's ways sat idle as this view from Way Six across to the mold loft and yard-office shows. (Marinship/Grambow, Pullin Collection.)

All the gantry cranes are perfectly aligned, awaiting the call to duty that never came. Many of the yard's buildings came down in the 1950s, as people tried to put the war behind them. Sausalito was no longer in the tanker business. (Marinship/Grambow, Pullin Collection.)

USS *Iowa* joined the fleet in February 1943, and spent most of World War II in the Pacific theater. In January 1945, *Iowa* returned to Hunters Point for overhaul, and was in dry dock until March 19. By April 4, the battleship was off Okinawa, supporting the invasion of that island and subsequently shelling the Japanese home islands. (Author's collection.)

Four

NAVAL SHIPYARDS

The Bay Area had two naval shipyards operating at the outbreak of World War II, Hunters Point and Mare Island. Hunters Point is located south of San Francisco, and Mare Island is located in the Carquinez Strait at the top of the bay. The Bay Area, a hub of the 1849 gold rush, saw a huge influx of ships bringing fortune seekers to the region. Ship repair and dismantling businesses naturally followed.

In 1867, the first commercial dry dock on the Pacific Coast opened at Potrero Point, later changed to Hunters Point, named after a local family. The Union Iron Works (later Bethlehem Shipbuilding) operated the dry dock and a pair of graving docks at the site.

In 1939, the U.S. Navy bought a 47-acre parcel for just under $4 million. In 1942, with America at war, the navy seized more than 100 homes surrounding Hunters Point to expand the base, and peak employment reached 18,000 in 1945. During the war, Hunters Point serviced hundreds of ships and was responsible for loading the components of "Little Boy," the first atom bomb dropped on Japan, onto the USS *Indianapolis* (CA-35). Having delivered the bomb parts to Tinian Island on July 26, 1945, the ship went missing in the Philippine Sea after being torpedoed by the Japanese submarine *I-58*. Of the *Indianapolis*'s 1,199-member crew, only 317 survived; most died in the water during the five days they awaited rescue. Hunters Point served through the Korean and Vietnam Wars and was used to test Polaris submarine-launched missiles during the cold war. The base closed in 1994.

Gen. Mariano Guadalupe Vallejo was deeded part of Rancho Soscol in 1844. The U.S. Navy acquired Mare Island from General Vallejo in July 1852, and two years later became the first U.S. Naval base on the West Coast. During World War II, Mare Island Naval Shipyard built 17 submarines, 4 submarine tenders, 31 destroyer escorts, 300 landing craft, and 33 other small ships. The destroyer *Ward* was built at Mare Island in only 17 and a half days from keel laying to launch. In addition to ships built at the facility, dozens more were overhauled or repaired throughout the war years. During World War II, more than 46,000 were employed at the facility. After building 17 nuclear submarines, including one named for General Vallejo, the facility was closed in 1996.

This is an aerial view of Hunters Point Naval Shipyard from 7,000 feet on May 24, 1945. Three of the dry docks are occupied, and an aircraft carrier is receiving attention from a floating crane in the center of the photograph. (National Archives, 40-1072M.)

A new 35-ton Washington Portal F-4 Crane is tested at Hunters Point on August 7, 1945. The boom is at its minimum radius and is being tested with an 87,500-pound load. This crane would later work the shipways, helping repair and overhaul ships from the Pacific theater. (National Archives, 40-1071M.)

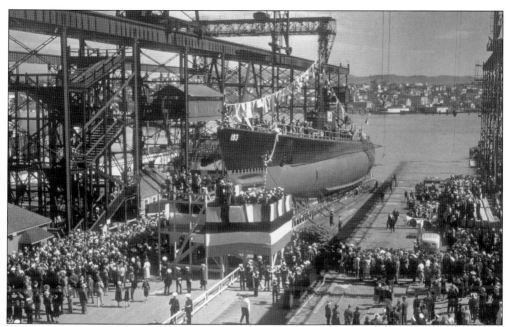

Mare Island Naval Shipyard built and overhauled a number of submarines during the war. Here *Swordfish* (SS-193) is launched with appropriate fanfare. *Swordfish* became the first American submarine credited with sinking a Japanese ship on December 15, 1941, when three torpedoes sent the 8,663-ton *Atsutusan Maru* to the bottom of the ocean near Hainan Island, China. SS-193 was lost south of Okinawa on January 12, 1945. (National Archives, 80GK-1379.)

The USS *Springer* (SS-414), left, is shown here on the building ways at Mare Island, January 3, 1944. *Spot*, (SS-413) is farther along on the right. By the end of the year, SS-414 had sunk four ships, rescued a dozen pilots, and downed three enemy planes. *Springer* was sold to Chile in 1972. (U.S. Navy via Navsource.org.)

After launching, SS-413 *Spot* is tied up to Mare Island's outfitting dock, on July 3, 1944. *Spot*'s periscope shears are scaffolded, and the forward torpedo doors are open to allow fresh air into the forward torpedo room while men work below deck. SS-413 entered the Yellow Sea off China in December 1944. On January 7, 1945, the ship began sinking Japanese shipping. After a number of years in storage, *Spot* was sold to Chile in 1974. (U.S. Navy via Navsource.org.)

The conning tower was a cramped place on a World War II fleet submarine. This is typical of the boats built at Mare Island and serviced at Hunters Point. (National Archives, 80GK-16013.)

The destroyer USS *Henley* (DD-391) was launched at Mare Island Navy Yard on January 12, 1937. *Henley* was at Pearl Harbor when the Japanese struck, and it is credited with downing one dive-bomber and shares credit with another ship for a second. On October 3, 1943, DD-391 was supporting operations in the waters off New Guinea, when it dodged a pair of torpedoes but was struck and sunk by a third. One officer and 14 men went missing. (Vallejo Naval and Historical Museum.)

British Destroyer Escort 14 (BDE-14) was launched as *Berry* on August 29, 1942, at Mare Island. Reclaimed by the U.S. Navy, the ship was named *Doherty* (DE-14) and commissioned on February 6, 1943. The vessel served primarily in Alaskan waters during the war. In December 1946, it was sold surplus and subsequently scrapped. (Vallejo Naval and Historical Museum.)

Mare Island-built Submarine Tender USS *Sperry* (AS-12) was named for inventor Elmer Sperry, noted for his gyroscopic compasses, and launched on December 17, 1941. AS-12 spent most of the war serving submarines from Pearl Harbor, Guam, and the Marianas. The ship served throughout the Korean and Vietnam Wars before being decommissioned in 1982. *Sperry* rests in the Suisun Bay Reserve Fleet in the hopes that it will someday soon become a floating museum. (Vallejo Naval and Historical Museum.)

Submarine Tender *Nereus* (AS-17) was the third ship to bear the name, which refers to the Greek god of the sea who was the eldest son of Pontus and Gaea and the father of 50 mermaids. This ship was laid down at Mare Island on October 11, 1943, and is seen here after being commissioned on October 27, 1945, too late to see service during World War II. (Vallejo Naval and Historical Museum.)

The tanker *Muir Woods* enters one of Mare Island's dry docks for post-delivery modifications.
(Vallejo Naval and Historical Museum.)

Abatan (AW-4) steams near Mare Island wearing what is known as Measure 32 (Design 7AO) camouflage. This ship was laid down at Marinship as *Mission San Lorenzo*, but was changed to AO-92 *Abatan* prior to launching on August 6, 1944. The ship was transferred to the navy and modified at Mare Island as a distilling ship. It provided freshwater to ships at Ulithi through the end of the war. (Vallejo Naval and Historical Museum.)

Early in the war, DD-250 *Lawrence*, escorted convoys between San Francisco, Seattle, and Alaska. In September 1942, the destroyer was based at Treasure Island, where it patrolled the approaches to the Golden Gate Bridge. On May 31, 1944, the *Lawrence* went to the aid of the Liberty Ship *Henry Bergh* (built at Kaiser Richmond, Yard No. 1), which was aground on the Farallon Islands. There it rescued 192 men. (Vallejo Naval and Historical Museum.)

Launched in April 1919, DD-208 *Hovey*, was nearing obsolescence when World War II broke out. Reconfigured as a high-speed minesweeper and designated DMS-11, *Hovey* served in the thick of combat at Guadalcanal. In 1943, it returned to Hunters Point for overhaul, and then joined a convoy sailing from Mare Island to New Caledonia. At the battle of Lingayen Gulf in the Philippines in January 1945, it was simultaneously struck by a Kamikaze plane and a torpedo. The ship sank, taking 48 souls with it. (Vallejo Naval and Historical Museum.)

After firing back at the Japanese during the Pearl Harbor raid, *Jarvis*, DD-393, patrolled Hawaiian waters for submarines. Having escorted a convoy to Australia, it returned to Mare Island to be updated. *Jarvis* left the West Coast for Australia and New Zealand and then participated in the first amphibious assault of the war at Guadalcanal. It was struck by a Japanese aerial torpedo during the battle. While making its way to Sidney for repairs, *Jarvis* was attacked and sunk with all hands on August 9, 1942. (Vallejo Naval and Historical Museum.)

Built at Mare Island in 1920, DD-339 *Trever* had been converted to a high-speed mine sweeper (DMS-16). Anchored at Pearl Harbor during the Japanese attack, *Trever* dispatched one Japanese plane. She returned to Mare Island at the beginning of 1942 to have her armament upgraded from four-inch guns to three-inch antiaircraft guns along with the addition of 20mm-antiaircraft cannons. (Vallejo Naval and Historical Museum.)

DD-392 was the second U.S. Navy ship to be named for Commodore Daniel Todd Patterson, defender of New Orleans against the British during the War of 1812. *Patterson* is seen after overhaul at Mare Island and about to depart for the invasion of the Solomon Islands. The ship was involved in nearly every major campaign in the Pacific, earning 13 battle stars for its service. (Vallejo Naval and Historical Museum.)

Monaghan, DD-354, rammed a midget submarine inside Pearl Harbor during the December 7, 1941, attack. Subsequently it was assigned to the Aleutian theater of combat were it was damaged in a collision in a heavy fog bank. After temporary repairs, the destroyer was sent to Mare Island for repair. *Monaghan* is seen here ready to return to combat duty. (Vallejo Naval and Historical Museum.)

Craven DD-382 spent most of the war escorting aircraft carriers in the major battles of the Pacific campaign. During the war, it was overhauled twice—once in April 1942 at Mare Island, and again at Hunters Point in September 1943. (Vallejo Naval and Historical Museum.)

The British light cruiser HMS *Liverpool's* bow was blown off by an Italian aircraft torpedo southeast of Crete in October 1940. The cruiser sailed nearly around the world for repairs at Mare Island. In addition, the light cruiser HMS *Orion* and other British ships were serviced at the shipyard. (Vallejo Naval and Historical Museum.)

Seen in the waters off Mare Island before the big battles of the Pacific, *Honolulu* (CL-48) would go on to sink a destroyer and a Sendai Class cruiser during the Battle of Kolombangara on July 13, 1943. (Vallejo Naval and Historical Museum.)

New Orleans (CA-32) participated in the Battle of the Coral Sea and the Battle of Midway. At Midway, where four Japanese carriers were sunk, the *New Orleans* rescued sailors from the torpedoed carrier Yorktown. Even though her bow was blown off by a torpedo during the Battle of Tassafaronga, the *New Orleans* was repaired to fight through the end of the war. (Vallejo Naval and Historical Museum.)

Attack Transport *Mendocino* (APA-100) transported troops to the Philippines for the invasion of Okinawa in the spring of 1945. After delivering more troops to Guam and Yokohama, it returned soldiers from the Pacific campaign to San Francisco as part of the Magic Carpet fleet. (Vallejo Naval and Historical Museum.)

Built at Bethlehem Shipbuilding of San Francisco, *Hazelwood* (DD-531) was launched on November 20, 1942. After a number of campaigns, *Hazelwood* was escorting a carrier group off Okinawa on April 29, 1945, when Kamikaze planes attacked the fleet. Hit by a Japanese Zero, 102 aboard the ship were killed. (Vallejo Naval and Historical Museum.)

Hazelwood proceeded to Mare Island, where this photograph was taken of her crumbled superstructure. Note that wartime censors have crosshatched out the ship's radar antenna in the upper left hand side of the photograph. It was estimated that it would take 350,000 man-hours to rebuild the ship. (Vallejo Naval and Historical Museum.)

This is an aerial view of the Mare Island waterfront after the war, with 47 submarines tied up in the foreground and Mount Diablo rising in the background. (Vallejo Naval and Historical Museum.)

Submarines fresh from patrol in the Pacific are docked at Mare Island. Many have begun the preservation process by having their propellers removed and placed on deck, and armament sealed under preservative coverings, as seen on SS-383 *Pampanito*. The second sub from the left in the back row is SS-282 *Tunny*, a Mare Island–built boat. Other identifiable boats include SS-196 *Searaven*, SS-241 *Bashaw*, SS-254 *Gurnard*, SS-261 *Mingo*, SS-375 *Macabi*, and SS-381 *Sand Lance*. (U.S. Navy.)

As preservation technologies changed, domes were added to protect the submarines from the elements. (Vallejo Naval and Historical Museum.)

On Armed Forces Day, SS-295 *Hackleback* was open for inspection by the public. *Hackleback* is moored between SS-412 *Trepang* on the left and *Sand Lance* on the right. (Vallejo Naval and Historical Museum.)

At the end of the war, *Perch* (SS-313) was decommissioned and placed in reserve at Hunters Point Naval Shipyard. Reactivated at Mare Island for the Korean War, Lt. Comdr. O. H. Payne took the ship to war for its second time. Lieutenant Commander Payne landed British Commandos near Tanchon, where they destroyed a train tunnel, with the loss of only one man. Payne was awarded the Bronze Star for bravery, the only submarine commander so decorated during the Korean War. (U.S. Navy.)

The Gato Class submarine *Tunny* (SS-282) was laid down on November 10, 1941, at Mare Island. The sub was launched on June 30, 1942, and entered service on September 1. Heavily damaged during her fourth war patrol by Japanese sub-chasers, *Tunny* returned to Hunters Point Naval Shipyard on September 17, 1943, for repairs. *Tunny* departed California on February 2, 1944, for its fifth war patrol. On March 23, 1944, *Tunny* sank the Japanese submarine *I-42* off the coast of Palau, in the Caroline Islands. After the war, SS-282 was stored at Mare Island. It was recommissioned SSG-282 on March 6, 1953, after modifications seen here, to carry and launch Regulus-guided missiles. (U.S. Navy.)

Pictured here are Moore Dry Dock–built 81 C2-S-B1 standard-cargo freighters, each displacing 4,682 tons. SS *Wild Wave* slid down the ways at Oakland on October 20, 1944. The C2-S-B1 freighters were 469 feet long, had a 63-foot beam, and were 40 feet deep, with a draft of 25 feet. They had a maximum speed of 15.5 knots. (Author's collection.)

Five

PENINSULA AND EAST BAY SHIPBUILDING

Shipbuilding in the San Francisco Bay Area benefited from the region's long maritime heritage, which, by World War II, was approaching 100 years. The experience local yards gained constructing ships during World War I put Bay Area yards at the forefront when the navy and U.S. Maritime Commission went looking for suitable builders for their new ship needs. The skilled labor pool of San Francisco, Oakland, and the surrounding suburbs enabled the yards to survive the Depression and to expand as the U.S. Maritime Commission began ramping up for the coming conflict.

Three major contributors to Bay Area shipbuilding were located along the Oakland-Alameda Estuary. They were Moore Dry Dock, Bethlehem Steel's Alameda operation, and United Engineering. Bethlehem Steel's Alameda yard built ships during World War I, and in World War II, 9,676-ton displacement Admiral Class troop transports (P2-SE2-R1), capable of carrying nearly 5,000 troops. Each ship was 608 feet long with a beam of 75 feet, 6 inches, and was powered by a pair of 18,000-horsepower turboelectric engines. Bethlehem-Alameda built seven of the transports, the last being AP-126 *Admiral Hugh Rodman*, commissioned July 10, 1945. Moore Dry Dock built 111 large ships for the navy and the U.S. Maritime Commission, ranging from C2 freighters to LSDs (Landing Ship Dock). United Engineering built 21 oceangoing Fleet Tugs for the U.S. Navy.

On the San Francisco Peninsula, Bethlehem San Francisco built 60 ships during World War II, ranging from destroyers and destroyer escorts to troopships and light cruisers. Farther down the peninsula, Barrett and Hilp built 19 concrete ships that were used as floating warehouses in the Pacific theater, and Western Pipe and Steel built 50 ships and 11 barges for the war effort. Western Pipe and Steel also converted four of its C3 freighters to escort aircraft carriers for the Royal Navy.

Each of these yards contributed a variety of ship types to the more than 1,000 ships built in the Bay Area during World War II.

Western Pipe and Steel, located in South San Francisco, built 44 transports of different types, four escort carriers, as well as one destroyer and one seaplane tender. Here the yard's employees gather for a war-bond drive. (South San Francisco Public Library Local History Collection.)

Raising money for the war effort was a major undertaking with each shift and each yard trying to outsell one another. Here winners of the Seventh War Loan bond sales contest gather in the Western Pipe and Steel Company offices. Pictured from left to right are Shirley Zimmer, first place; Jean Murman, Seventh War Loan sales contest chairwoman; Jim Anderson, second place; Frank Carnesecca, sixth place; and Jake Masden, superintendent of Western Pipe and Steel shipyard. (South San Francisco Public Library Local History Collection.)

"Loose Lips Might Sink Ships" was one of the many wartime posters adorning the walls of the shipyards encouraging workers to keep what they know to themselves. (National Archives.)

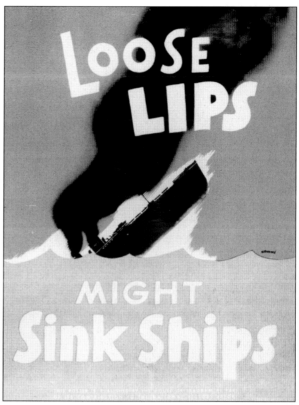

Pacific Coast Engineering of Alameda built Baby Liberty transverse bulkheads and other subassemblies for Kaiser's Richmond Yard No. 4. A stern section can be seen to the rear. (Richmond Museum of History Collection.)

Mrs. Frank P. Lucas breaks a bottle of champagne across the bow of SS *Neptune's Car*, a C-2-S-B1–type freighter built at Moore Dry Dock Company, in Oakland, on April 21, 1944. (Oakland Public Library.)

The U.S. Maritime Commission had contracted for 26 concrete ships to be built by Barrett and Hilp Shipyards of South San Francisco. Here the steel framework for the hull is positioned, much like rebar used in other building work. Each of the concrete ships, actually an engineless barge, took six to eight weeks to build, could carry 6,000 tons, and cost $600,000 to construct. The first of Barrett and Hilp's barges was launched in June 1943. (South San Francisco Public Library Local History Collection.)

This is a bow view of a Barrett and Hilp concrete ship showing the hatches and the beginning of the midships deckhouse. Note the workers in the scaffolding at the bow. (South San Francisco Public Library Local History Collection.)

These workers are outfitting the concrete ships to serve as floating warehouses. Ventilators will allow air to circulate in the holds. (South San Francisco Public Library Local History Collection.)

Workers and guests gathered at Belair Shipyard to witness the launching of its 19th concrete ship, *Cinnabar*, on March 10, 1944. At the same ceremony, the U.S. Maritime Commission's "M" Award was presented to the yard. Sponsor of the new ship was Mrs. Flesher, wife of Carl W. Flesher, director of the Maritime Commission's West Coast Regional Office. The barge at the far left is *Marl*, and second from left is *Barite*, the 16th and 17th ships, respectively, built at South San Francisco. (South San Francisco Public Library Local History Collection.)

The U.S. Maritime Commission contracted with Western Pipe and Steel for the diesel-powered, 6,778-ton C1-B freighter *American Manufacturer*. The ship was side launched into the San Francisco Bay on August 8, 1940, as seen here, and was delivered on April 11, 1941. (South San Francisco Public Library Local History Collection.)

American Manufacturer settles on the once-calm bay waters. Notice the large amount of floating debris formerly used to hold the ship to the way. (South San Francisco Public Library Local History Collection.)

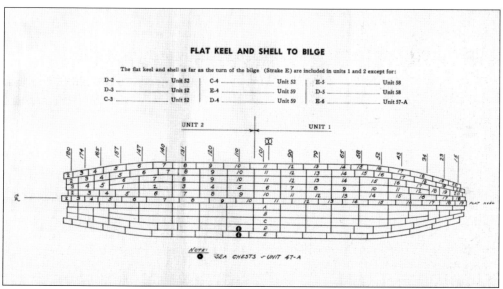

Pictured is a keel-plate diagram for a C3 freighter as built by Western Pipe and Steel. These hulls were also converted to escort carriers for the British. Once the keel or flat keel was laid, the double bottom was lowered into place, allowing workers to mount the engine bed and begin positioning the transverse bulkheads. (Author's collection.)

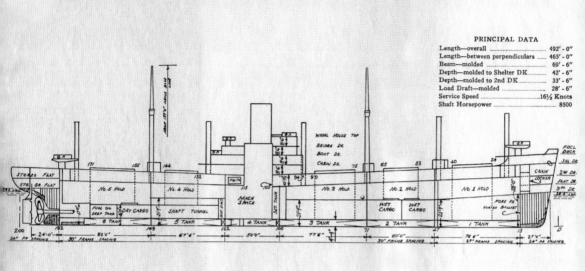

This is a side profile of a C3 cargo vessel showing the layout of the holds, deck spaces, and cargo compartments. (Author's collection.)

Sea Starling, a C3-S-A4 freighter, was launched on March 6, 1945, and delivered on June 12, 1946, too late to see service in World War II. It was one of the last three ships launched by Western Pipe and Steel. The U.S. Maritime Commission sold the ship to American President Lines, which operated it as *President Madison* until 1972. (South San Francisco Public Library Local History Collection.)

The U.S. Maritime Commission originally ordered 12 EC-2 steam engines, but the order kept increasing as the need for ships expanded. The men and women of Joshua Hendy Iron Works eventually built 754 Liberty-ship engines, or nearly 30 percent of the engines needed for the Liberty fleet. The jubilant workers are shown delivering the last EC-2 engine on April 2, 1945. (The Iron Man Museum, JH4991.)

Six

SHIP ENGINES
IN THE SOUTH BAY

Shortly after the gold rush of 1849, the Joshua Hendy Iron Works began building mining equipment in San Francisco. The company's factory was destroyed in the 1906 San Francisco Earthquake and fire, and the business was relocated to Sunnyvale, at the southern end of San Francisco Bay. Hendy did well until the Depression struck in 1929.

By 1940, the Hendy Iron Works had gone into receivership and was being operated by the Bank of California. At this point, Charlie Moore, owner of the Moore Machinery Company, was dealing the Hendy Company. He saw that the company was on the ropes and contacted Felix Kahn of MacDonald and Kahn. Moore realized Hendy's equipment could be sold off for more than the sum of the company and approached Kahn to help buy the firm. A deal was struck, and the partners of the Six Companies were offered shares. Henry J. Kaiser bought 7.5 percent, as did a number of the other partners. Kahn acquired 17.5 percent, and Charlie Moore controlled the company with 35 percent.

Securing $10 million in contracts from the navy to build torpedo launchers, the company was back on its feet. Through Henry J. Kaiser, Hendy got into the Liberty-ship-engine business, eventually building 754 of the steam-driven, triple-expansion engines. The facility also built turbine engines for Victory ships. Wartime expansion saw the plant grow from 146,000 square feet to more than 1.25 million. At peak employment, nearly 7,500 workers entered the plant each day.

After the war, Six Companies partners John McCone and Stephen Bechtel decided to buy out the other Hendy partners. McCone refocused the company, working on navy-ordnance projects and the U.S. Air Force's Tullahoma (Tennessee) axial-flow wind-tunnel compressor, as well as on building printing and binding equipment for *Time* magazine. In November 1946, McCone and Bechtel sold the business to Westinghouse (now Lockheed Martin), which operates its Marine Division at the plant. The Lockheed Martin operation continues the 60-plus years of nautical traditions of the Joshua Hendy Iron Works and its Sunnyvale factory.

The EC-2 Liberty-ship steam engine featured three cylinders at the top of the engine, a high-pressure cylinder (24.5 inches in diameter), an intermediate-pressure cylinder (37 inches), and a low-pressure cylinder (70 inches). The engine's stroke was 48 inches, and it could develop 2,500 horsepower to propel the ship at 11 knots. (The Iron Man Museum.)

This is a side view of a Hendy-built, triple-expansion steam engine for Liberty ships, seen on the shop floor on October 23, 1943. (The Iron Man Museum, JH2142.)

Shown here is an aerial view of the Hendy plant in Sunnyvale during the war years. Notice the large number of orchards that surround the plant. This is not a location one would expect for the largest ship-engine builder during the war. (The Iron Man Museum.)

Each engine produced the 2,500 horsepower needed to drive the ship's propeller. Compare the size of the engine assemblies to the size of the men working to fit each piece of this Liberty-ship engine. (The Iron Man Museum.)

Virginia Azarello is working on a turbine-engine stator. This photograph was used to recognize Azarello as Hendy's "Iron Woman" of the month for June 1943. Hendy had special hats designed to accommodate women's hair and to prevent accidents while looking stylish. (The Iron Man Museum, JH-1253.)

These workers are assembling turbines for Victory-ship engines on the factory floor, May 1944. (The Iron Man Museum.)

These workers are checking the tolerances on a C-1 double-reduction gear at the Hendy factory. (The Iron Man Museum.)

Significant milestones in production at Hendy were marked with a group gathering and photograph, used not only to commemorate the occasion but to boost worker morale. (The Iron Man Museum, JH-2138.)

Joshua Hendy built Mark 14 quintuple-torpedo-tube mounts for combat ships at its Sunnyvale plant. The torpedo trainer would sit on the bench above the tubes and hand-crank the mount in azimuth, using the round wheels with handgrips, seen to the left of the No. 79 sign. Under the sign is the torpedo-gyro-setting hand crank, and below that is the depth-setting mechanism. (The Iron Man Museum, JH-5169.)

The Battleship *Iowa* (BB-61) sits in the Suisun Bay Reserve Fleet awaiting a decision on its future home port. Two Northern California groups have put forth proposals to preserve the ship as a museum and monument to those who have served in the U.S. Navy. (Nicholas A. Veronico.)

Seven

PRESERVING
THE LEGACY

Fortunately the Bay Area's rich maritime heritage is not confined to books or a few fading memories. More than 1,000 ships were built in the region during the World War II, and a number have been preserved—some fully operational—to show new generations their history and how they operated.

After the war, huge numbers of Libertys and other ships were stored in the Bay Area, at Hunters Point, Mare Island, and in the waters of Suisun Bay, which were home to excess military shipping in the decades following the war. Hunters Point and Mare Island were active shipyards for more than four decades after the end of war and saw thousands of workers carry on the traditions of the World War II shipbuilders.

The Bay Area has not forgotten its wartime maritime heritage, and a number of ships have been preserved here, including the SS *Jeremiah O'Brien*, a Liberty based in San Francisco; the *Red Oak Victory*, which was returned to its birthplace in Richmond; the submarine USS *Pompanito*, which was serviced here during the war, was stored at Mare Island after V-J Day, and is now displayed along the San Francisco waterfront; the aircraft carrier USS *Hornet*, which was a hero of the battles in the Pacific, later played a highly visible role in the Apollo Moon missions, and is now in Alameda; and Franklin D. Roosevelt's yacht, the *Potomac*. These ships all serve as reminders of the thousands that were a part of the shipping industry in the Bay Area during World War II.

In 2007, there are still a number of cargo-carrying Victory ships, as well as a Marinship-built tanker, a Mare Island–built submarine tender, and an LST (Landing Ship, Tank) tied up in the Suisun Bay Reserve Fleet. Whether they will be preserved as museum ships is yet to be determined; however, it would be great to see the Mare Island–built submarine tender *Sperry* (AS-12), or the *Mission Santa Ynez*, the last surviving Marinship tanker, returned for display where they were built.

The last unaltered Liberty ship, the SS *Jeremiah O'Brien*, operates from the San Francisco waterfront. During World War II, the ship made 11 trips to bring supplies and equipment in support of the D-Day landings. In 1994, for the 50th anniversary of D-Day, volunteers sailed the ship through the Panama Canal to Portsmouth, England, and on to the commemoration. (Nicholas A. Veronico.)

The meticulously restored bridge of the SS *Jeremiah O'Brien* is open for tours. The ship makes a number of cruises on the bay and runs its triple-expansion steam engines on nine weekends each year (www.ssjeremiahobrien.org). (Nicholas A. Veronico.)

The only preserved Richmond-built Victory ship is the *Red Oak Victory* (see page 24), which is now berthed at Richmond Yard No. 3, Berth 6A. Here the ship is seen shortly after emerging from the reserve fleet at the beginning of its restoration and tied up at Richmond's Terminal One. Tours of the ship are currently conducted as volunteers work to restore *Red Oak Victory* to fully operational status (www.ssredoakvictory.org). (Nicholas A. Veronico.)

The World War II Balao Class submarine *Pampanito* (SS-383) is open to the public at Pier 45 in Fisherman's Wharf. Dozens of submarines, from diesel to nuclear boats, were built at San Francisco Bay's Mare Island, and *Pampanito* serves as a monument to those who built and served aboard submarines. It is also the only World War II submarine open for inspection on the West Coast (www.maritime.org/pamphome.htm). (Nicholas A. Veronico.)

The presidential yacht *Potomac* sails on the San Francisco Bay during Fleet Week with the Richmond-San Rafael Bridge in the background. The former yacht of Pres. Franklin D. Roosevelt has been restored and is open for tours in Oakland's Jack London Square. The ship also makes a number of cruises on the bay each year (www.usspotomac.org). (Nicholas A. Veronico.)

The bows of five World War II–vintage Victory ships can be seen past the stern of LST-1158 *Tioga County* in the Suisun Bay Reserve Fleet. Closest to the camera is *Hannibal Victory*, then *Pan Am Victory* (both from Richmond Yard No. 2), *Occidental Victory*, *Rider Victory*, and in the distance *Sioux Falls Victory* (all three built at Calship). *Hannibal Victory*, *Occidental Victory*, and *Sioux Falls Victory* were sold to ship breakers in the fall of 2006. (Nicholas A. Veronico.)

LST-1158 *Tioga County* saw extensive service during the Vietnam War, most notably repositioning the 101st Airborne Division to Tuy Hoa in January 1966. Today *Tioga County* sits among dozens of other ships in the Suisun Bay Reserve Fleet with the hopes that a veterans group will preserve it. Only two LSTs have been preserved—one in Michigan (LST-393) and the other in Indiana (LST-325). (Nicholas A. Veronico.)

Currently two groups are attempting to acquire the Battleship *Iowa* for display. A group in Stockton, California, has backing from the Port of Stockton, which plans to transfer Berth 14 at Rough and Ready Island along with a 90,000-square-foot building for museum use. In Vallejo, the Historic Ships Memorial at Pacific Square (HSMPS) has plans to berth the *Iowa* at Mare Island. The U.S. Navy is currently reviewing proposals from both groups. (Nicholas A. Veronico.)

USS *Hornet* (www.uss-hornet.org), now berthed in Alameda, California, saw extensive service during World War II, with its pilots downing 1,410 Japanese aircraft. This ship also recovered the Apollo 11 and Apollo 12 capsules after splash-down in the Pacific. Pres. Richard Nixon was on board to welcome the Apollo 11 crew home. Exhibits of the ship's history, including the Apollo recoveries, as well as historic naval aircraft, can be viewed aboard the ship. (Roger Cain.)

BIBLIOGRAPHY

Bonnett, Wayne. *Build Ships! Wartime Shipbuilding Photographs San Francisco Bay: 1940–1945.* Sausalito, CA: Windgate Press, 1999.

Bastin, Donald. *Images of America: Richmond (California).* San Francisco: Arcadia Publishing, 2003.

Del French, Chauncey. *Waging War on the Home Front.* Corvallis, OR: Oregon State University Press, 2004.

Finnie, Richard. *Marinship: The History of a Wartime Shipyard.* San Francisco: Marinship Corporation, 1947.

Gayer, George F. *The Iron Men of Hendy.* Sunnyvale, CA: Iron Man Museum, 1985.

Heiner, Albert. *Henry J. Kaiser: Western Colossus.* San Francisco: Halo Books, 1991.

Houlihan, James. *Western Shipbuilders in World War II.* Oakland: Shipbuilding Review Publishing Association, 1945.

Jaffee, Capt. Walter W. *The Liberty Ships: From A to Z.* Palo Alto, CA: The Glencannon Press, 2004.

———. *The Victory Ships: From A to Z.* Palo Alto, CA: The Glencannon Press, 2006.

Kesselman. Amy. *Fleeting Opportunities: Women Shipyard Workers in Portland and Vancouver during World War II and Reconversion.* Albany, NY: State University of New York Press, 1990.

Lane, Frederic C. *Ships for Victory: A History of Shipbuilding under the U.S. Maritime Commission in World War II.* Baltimore, MD: The Johns Hopkins Press, 1951.

Lemmon, Sue and E. D. Wichels. *Sidewheelers to Nuclear Power: A Pictorial Essay Covering 123 Years at the Mare Island Naval Shipyard.* Vallejo, CA: Mare Island Naval Shipyard, 1977.

Mawdsley, Dean L. *Steel Ships and Iron Pipe.* San Francisco, CA: Associates of the National Maritime Museum Library at The Glencannon Press, 2002.

Sawyer, L. A. and W. H. Mitchell. *Victory Ships and Tankers.* Newton Abbot, England: David & Charles, 1974.

———. *The Liberty Ships* (Second Edition). New York: Lloyd's of London Press, 1985.

Veronico, Nicholas A. and Armand H. Veronico. *Battlestations: American Warships of World War II.* St. Paul, MN: MBI Publishing Company, 2001.

Wollenberg, Charles. *Marinship at War.* Berkeley, CA: Western Heritage Press, 1990.

Fore 'n' Aft. Kaiser Shipyards, Richmond, CA. Various issues.

The Marin-er. Marinship, Sausalito, CA. Various issues.

ACROSS AMERICA, PEOPLE ARE DISCOVERING SOMETHING WONDERFUL. *THEIR HERITAGE.*

Arcadia Publishing is the leading local history publisher in the United States. With more than 3,000 titles in print and hundreds of new titles released every year, Arcadia has extensive specialized experience chronicling the history of communities and celebrating America's hidden stories, bringing to life the people, places, and events from the past. To discover the history of other communities across the nation, please visit:

www.arcadiapublishing.com

Customized search tools allow you to find regional history books about the town where you grew up, the cities where your friends and family live, the town where your parents met, or even that retirement spot you've been dreaming about.

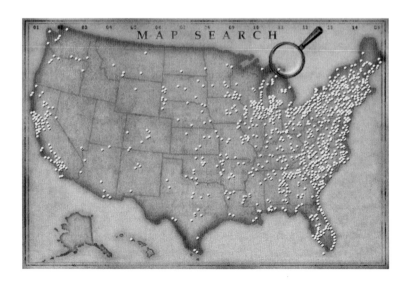